—WIND—MOUNTAIN—OAK—

Tupelo Press Poetry in Translation

Abiding Places: Korea, South and North, by Ko Un
Translated from Korean by Hillel Schwartz and Sunny Jung

Invitation to a Secret Feast: Selected Poems, by Joumana Haddad
Translated from Arabic by Khaled Mattawa with the poet, and with Najib
Awad, Issa Boullata, Marilyn Hacker, Henry Matthews, and David Harsent

Night, Fish and Charlie Parker, by Phan Nhien Hao
Translated from Vietnamese by Linh Dinh

Stone Lyre: Poems of René Char
Translated from French by Nancy Naomi Carlson

This Lamentable City: Poems of Polina Barskova
Translated from Russian by Ilya Kaminsky and others

New Cathay: Contemporary Chinese Poetry 1990–2012
Edited by Ming Di and translated from Chinese by several hands

Ex-Voto, by Adelia Prado
Translated from Brazilian Portuguese by Ellen Dore Watson

Gossip and Metaphysics: Russian Modernist Poems and Prose
Edited by Katie Farris, Ilya Kaminsky, and Valzhyna Mort, with translations
by the editors and others

Calazaza's Delicious Dereliction, by Suzanne Dracius
Translated from French by Nancy Naomi Carlson with the poet

Canto General: Song of the Americas, by Pablo Neruda
Translated from Spanish by Mariela Griffor and Jeffrey Levine

Hammer with No Master, by René Char
Translated from French by Nancy Naomi Calrson

A Certain Roughness in Their Syntax, by Jorge Auliciano
Translated from Spanish by Judith Filc with the poet

Xeixa: Fourteen Catalan Poets
Edited and translated from Catalan by Marlon L. Fick and Francisca Esteve

—WIND—MOUNTAIN—OAK—

THE POEMS OF SAPPHO

TRANSLATED BY DAN BEACHY-QUICK

Tupelo Press
North Adams, Massachusetts

Wind—Mountain—Oak: The Poems of Sappho
Copyright © 2023 Dan Beachy Quick. All rights reserved.

Library of Congress Control Number: 2022949983

ISBN: 978-1-946482-81-5 (paperback)
ISBN: 979-8-379309-32-9 (hardcover)

Cover and text design by Bill Kuch.

Cover art: East pediment of the Parthenon, figures L & M, circa 432BCE.
British Museum 1816,0610.97

Based on the edition Greek Lyric, Volume I: Sappho and Alcaeus
Edited by David A. Campbell. Harvard University Press, 1982
Loeb Classical Library #142

First edition June 2023

Tupelo Press
P.O. Box 1767
North Adams, Massachusetts 01247
413-664-9611 / Fax: 413-664-9711
editor@tupelopress.org
www.tupelopress.org

Tupelo Press is an award-winning independent literary press
that publishes fine fiction, non-fiction, and poetry
in books that are a joy to hold as well as read.
Tupelo Press is a registered 501(c)(3) nonprofit organization, and
we rely on public support to carry out our mission of publishing
extraordinary work that may be outside the realm of large commercial
publishers. Financial donations are welcome and are tax deductible.

Table of Contents

—for Rebecca Beachy & Liz Weinstein
...the pale light that each upon the other throws.

OF SAPPHO

These are the songs she sang. Hymns of invocation singing into precence gods astray in their holy seclusions. Aphrodite from Cyprus. Artemis from the mountains running with deer in the woods. Invocations of rivers. Thought is flow. Invocations of meadows. Thought is a flower. Songs of the dances of rivers and meadows. Love songs singing youth's beauty. Hymen songs. Wedding songs. The rites of Aphrodite. Singing on the lyre, she goes to the bridal chamber, hangs garlands around the room, roses woven in the garlands, she brings young women into the bedroom, she brings in Aphrodite and braids hyacinth through her hair, save for a loose strand on the forehead of the goddess for the breeze to blow. These are the songs she sings. Jealousy of the lover's eye turned to another. Lust-songs and songs of fear. Complaint and rueful longing. Songs to pass the time while weaving. Songs that, plaiting tender stem to tender stem, make a green eternal crown. Song of the bride's beautiful feet. Song of the purple hem. Brighter than bright. More golden than gold. Song of the loosening sash. Bleating song of the goat pure white. Song of the tragic gift. Sings the pain of the nightingale's clear tone. A dress. An anklet. The wandering stars. A necklace. A bracelet. The moon. Song of the apple high in the tree. Faith in fragile luxuries. Song of the golden rings.

Sappho teaches us that an ankle glimpsed beneath the hem of a dress is a cosmological fact as central to the work of the world as are the dangling lights of stars, those earrings in the vast dark. A foot slipped into a sandal finely sewn is a law as natural and necessary to the order of the world as is the orbit of the planets. It is there in the word itself: κόσμος World-order, universe. Rule of the fixed system. Stars. The seven planets. But *cosmos* also means adornment. *Cosmos* also means praise. Sappho teaches us that a love song clasps itself around the object of its adoration just as a necklace clasps around a neck, gold warming to the heat of the skin, pendant pulsing with the pulse; she teaches us the moon is only the visible clasp of the unseen, finely forged, necklace that encircles the earth. Among the most ancient lessons these poems might offer is that the erotic isn't merely the amorous needs of the nerves—the erotic is an epistemology. Desire calls out, and when someone responds to that call, when that person stands before us, the sheer fact of her presence shatters us. Shining face and honey-voice. To see that we are also seen…it snaps us from the mere inward elf-involvement of minor wants and imagined fantasies, and puts us also in the world, responsible to who and what we love.

Though it might not seem so at first, reading Sappho's poetry does in us as serious a philosophic work as does reading Anaximander, an early thinker writing in Miletus at the same time Sappho was singing in Lesbos. He thought the fundamental source of the world is the *apeiron*, boundlessness, and that infinite worlds were infinitely being born and, like an endless elegy, infinitely dying. Thales, too, lived during Sappho's life—man who first understood the motions of the stars, who read the astrological signs, who reaped profit from the pressing of olives, and who thought water was the origin of all. The third of the great pre-Socratic philosophers, Anaximenes, was a student of Anaximander during Sappho's years. He thought about the air. That all was born from air, even the gods. That the three thinkers on the western coast of Turkey who gave rise to what would become philosophy lived concurrently with Sappho who, on an island in the far east of the Aegean Sea, very near Miletus, created what we know as lyric poetry, feels less a coincidence than a cosmic harmony. We might remember a mythological fact fallen into the oblivion of the modern mind's arrogance: that the nine Muses were sisters, born of Force and Memory, insisting that Astronomy, Love Poems, Song, Tragedy, Comedy, Dance, History, Epic, and Sacred Hymns are all but a singular Music. Before philosophy became Philosophy, we had more simply *philos* and *sophos*, *love* and *wisdom*, each simultaneous and separate—Sappho's simple, urgent, "Atthis: you;" and Thales falling into a hole while looking up at the stars. Less an emotion than a cosmological fact, Sappho might remind us about love's deeper nature. First there was Chaos and there was also Earth, and Eros brought them together. Day was born. And the sky. The stars and hills. Sappho, known throughout antiquity as the "tenth Muse," sings of love in its ache and ecstasy, its agony and its refuge, as if love were the binding force holding the world together. Maybe it is. Even the gods shudder when they feel it—love.

Time is love's lament. Love says no to the morning sun, but the sun rises. For years every day the sun rises. Time says no to old age, but as the poet Theognis reminds us, life's "slow weight gathers; old age suddenly stands up inside you."

The poet seeks, as Sappho puts it, "fame never dying." The poem is meant to keep the one who is loved free from time's ravages, recognizable across centuries, a splendor millennia cannot dull, some ongoing present tense that is as close to eternity as we can come, at home in the life of another's mind not yet born:

> Someone keeps us in mind
> I say
> in time yet to come

Our minds are those "yet to come," suddenly here, not that we can explain the mystery of it to ourselves, alive with the quick nerve of another's thought. But nothing is whole. We do not have the grace of the lovely woman walking; we have instead the stone fragment of her ankle. We do not have the lovely young man pouring wine in a golden bowl; we have the porcelain crook of an elbow, no more. But, as in the finest statuary, one can see the marble vein beneath marble skin, even these mere fragments pulse with life. It is a life time has hammered apart; but in every part, the heart still hammers.

*

Armies gather and disappear, cities rise from stone and return to rubble, deathless kings die, even the gods must go missing, to explain how we lose a poem to time. A library burns to the ground.

No one knows with any certainty what the Great Library of Alexandria looked like, but there are rumors. Modeled on Plato's Old Academy, there was a building dedicated to the Muses, a *Museum*; near the Museum, the Library itself, comprised of multiple wings, lines of shelves in covered walkways, rooms specific to the study of one author or specific academic pursuits. There were classrooms in which the scholars would occasionally teach. The Great Library may have held as many as 700,000 scrolls and books. A Second Library, a branch or "daughter," housed in the Temple of Serapis, held another 40,000 volumes. This library was known as the *Sarapeion*. The seed of the Library, so it is said, came from Alexander the Great himself, who donated the volumes his teacher Aristotle prepared for him. Knowledge is a form of lust that wants to gather more knowledge around it. The Ptolemaic kings (Soter, Philadelphus) who ruled Egypt supported the Library's acquisitions, decreeing that any book brought to Alexandria, by boat or by caravan, would be taken from its owners and copied by scribes. The copy would be returned; the original given to the Library. Eventually, they scoured the Mediterranean entire for books, scrolls, texts of every kind, and placed them in the Library. The poet Callimachus, who may or may not have been a librarian at the Great Library (living tax-free in royal quarters, eating at a common table with other scholars), created the first catalog system, the *Pinakes*, or "Tables." One of the categories, *From the boats*, marked stolen books. There were other categories. *Poetry*, among them. The catalog comprised 120 volumes, each volume gone missing.

In 48BC, fleeing the Civil Wars in Rome, Pompey the Great fled to Egypt, seeking refuge. He did not find it. The 13-year old Ptolemy XIII sent a fishing boat with three soldiers to escort Pompey to shore. They stabbed him to death. Cut off his head. Took off his clothes. Threw his naked body in the sea. A few days later, Julius Caesar arrived. He sought victory. He was given Pompey's head, and turned away in disgust. He was given Pompey's ring, and he wept. He sent what remains he could to Pompey's wife, Cornelia, and stayed in Alexandria.

Twenty two warships arrived in the wharf, in support of the deceased Pompey. Caesar set fire to them all. And the fire spread: ships to warehouses, warehouses to city, city to the Great Library, which burned to the ground. The Daughter lived; the Mother perished.

For six more centuries the *Sarapeion* held books scholars travelled to find, though over time royal support diminished, and the glory of the Great Library remained only in tatters. In 641CE Emir Amrou Ibn el-As took

Alexandria, and finding no books in accordance with the teachings of Allah, burned the remaining pages to heat the baths. It took six months to empty the library, six months before the waters cooled. So we are left with forgotten names in cold water.

The only books to survive, so it is said, were those with which the library began, Aristotle's teachings, written down for a man to learn what he could learn, so he could conquer the world.

*

Sappho wrote nine books of poetry. All were lost in the fires of Alexandria—either in the conflagration of Caesar's flames, or page by page later. But given Sappho's poems, their domestic concern, their turning away from epic and epic's battles to bridal chambers and the bliss of the nuptial bed, it makes a poetic sense that her poems fueled the waters of the baths. So I imagine it, though I doubt it is true. Of those nine books, we have now only a few complete poems; torn fragments of others; and of others, a few words, or one word, is all that remains. They are found in the middens of ancient Egyptian cities, among the scraps of papyrus—receipts, ledger-pages, poems—used in *cartonnage*, the *papier-mâché*-like construction method by which the mummies' sarcophagi were made. Scholiasts and the *Suda*. Strabo's *Geography*. Second century papyri "commentaries." Ancient books on meter and literary styles. These are the remnants, most no larger than a swatch of cloth from a wedding dress, by which we know Sappho. Photius's *Lexicon*. Pollux's *Vocabulary*. Lines scribbled on the shards of pots. Quotations in letters. Rumors passed from ear to ear for thousands of years:

> Solon of Athens, son of Execestides, when his nephew sang a song of Sappho's over the wine, liked the song and told the boy to teach it to him; and when someone asked why he was so eager about it, he said, "So that I may learn it and die."

3

Of her life we know little. Some gossip, some jokes, few facts. Born on Lesbos in the city of Mytilene. Her father had many names, but most agree on a version of Scamander or Scamandronymus. Her mother has but a single name, Cleis—the same name Sappho gives to her daughter. She lost her parents at an early age. Three brothers. The eldest, Charaxus, traded wine, and fell under the spell of a courtesan, Doricha, upon whom he wasted fortunes. He ended up roaming "the dark blue seas with agile oar," stealing from others the wealth he had lost himself. She seems to have admired most her youngest brother, Larichus, who poured out wine for wealthy patrons. Of the other brother, Erigyius, we learn only that he wore nice clothes. She might have had a husband; or, for the famously woman-loving poet, a husband might have been added to her, a malicious joke played by a satirist that millennia now has perpetuated. His name was Cercylas, a trader from Andros—a name that translates as "All-Cock" from the island of Man. But Sappho loved women. Her dearest friends—Atthis, Telesippa, and Megara—were also her lovers. She taught poetry to other women, Gongyla, Eunica, and Anagora among them—love poems and hymns.

Her appearance is described in unflattering ways, but Plato called her beautiful and wise. And the Mytileneans stamped her face on their coins. Song the oldest currency. She left Mytilene in exile to Sicily sometime between the years 605-591, though no one seems to know why—perhaps a political fallout with the Cleanactidai family then ruling Lesbos. She returned home during the rule of the tyrant Pittacus, who came to power after challenging the general of the attacking Athenian army to single combat and killing him by sword, saving many lives. Home in Lesbos, Sappho surrounded herself with young women—some say forming a finishing school for girls soon to be married; others saying she formed a cult worshipping Aphrodite. No one knows. Both and neither are true.

Both and neither are true, as are the stories of her death. Sappho, from antiquity through the Middle Ages to now, has simultaneously been celebrated for the exquisite sensuality of her poetry and reviled for the morals of the life that led to the poems. Men who lived hundreds of years after the poet accused her of prostitution, of licentiousness, of corrupting the young women around her. Others gave her a husband she might never have had. Even the story of her death becomes a way of moralizing her life into a more acceptable, heterosexual, shape. And though some say she died in her old age, another story is the one more often told.

It is said she fell in love with a man named Phaon. Of him, there are also many stories. Some say he was loved by Aphrodite, too, who gave him youth and beauty after the decent old man ferried her in his boat for free; the goddess transformed him, and hid him among lettuces. Others say he was a fisherman who found a plant known as "sea-holly," whose root comes in the shape of male and female genitals. The man who finds a phallic root becomes irresistible. In either version, Phaon isn't simply a handsome man. He is magical, erotically magnetic, god-charged. Stories say that Sappho loved this god-loved man. That love shattered her as wind shatters pine. That love drove her mad. It isn't to be believed, only told. Strabo describes her death:

> {The island of Leucas contains} the temple of Apollo Leucates and the leap believed to cure love; 'where they say that Sappho first,' as Meander puts it, 'hunting the haughty Phaon, threw herself in her goading desire from the far-seen cliff...' Meander, then, says that Sappho was the first to leap, but those more skilled in antiquarian lore say it was Cephalus, son of Deioneus, enamoured of Pterelas. It was a custom among the Leucadians each year at the festival of Apollo that some criminal be thrown from the look-out for the sake of averting evil; all kinds of wings and birds were fastened to him in an effort to break his fall by their fluttering, and many people in small fishing boats waite d in a circle below and did what they could to rescue the man and take him to safety beyond the borders.

*

So it is we find ourselves among those many in their fishing boats, doing all we can to save the life of the poet who jumped into the sea. I can imagine books tied to her back like swan's wings; I can see poems, lines, words, pinned to her robe like feathers. Homer says words are winged. But even as I picture it, nothing slows her fall. But from the dark sea's depths some words and lines float up to the surface of the waves. The body has gone missing, but if we gather all we can, and weave them together as the poet weaved once her garlands, then we've rescued something of her, saved what we can save—have translated her beyond the borders, into what safety any of us in the end can have. Another heart's harbor. The port of a living mind.

PERSONAE
(some in the poems,
some lost to time)

Adonis—a god of beauty and desire. Child of the incestuous relationship between Theias, King of Syria, and his daughter Myyrha, who tricked him into sleeping with her. Myyrha gave birth to Adonis while transformed into a myrrh tree, a metamorphosis to protect her from her father wrath. Aphrodite gave the child to Persephone to raise. As a man he spent one third of the year in the underworld, another third with Love herself, and chose with whom to spend the last 4 months—most often, Aphrodite. He died while hunting. A wild boar killed him—sent by a jealou s god, Artemis or Ares.

Anactoria—friend and lover.

Anagora—friend, lover, student.

Andromache—wife of Hector, mother to Astynax, baby thrown to his death from a tower of Troy.

Andromeda—a rival poet.

Aphrodite—goddess of erotic Love. Born of sea foam. Chariot pulled by sparrows or doves. Or rides on the wings of swan. Unfaithful wife of Hephaestus. Also known as *Cytherea* and *Cypris*, in recognition of two lands that claim themselves as birthplace of the deity.

Apollo—god of prophecy and poetry, god of medicine and arrows and sun.

Artemis—virgin goddess of the hunt in the wild woods. Protector of young women. Protector of childbirth.

Atthis—friend and lover.

Cercylas—a wealthy trader, and Sappho's husband. Potentially a joke from a satirist. "All-Cock."

Charaxus—Sappho's eldest brother. Some say he lived on Lesbos, in the city of Mytilene; others in Egypt, in Naucratis. Made his living importing Lesbian wine. Spent vast sums of money on his mistress, Doricha, including contributing to her tomb. Others say he lost his entire fortune and, aflame with love for Doricha, angered by his sister's good advice, he roamed the seas, seeking ill-gotten money.

Cleis—Sappho's mother

Cleis—Sappho's daughter, named after Sappho's mother.

Doricha—(also called Rhodopis) a slave freed by Charaxus, who became both his mistress and a famous courtesan. Sappho thought she stole money from her brother.

Erigyius—Sappho's third brother. A fragment mentions the beauty of his clothes.

Gongyla—friend, lover, student.

Gorgo—a rival poet.

Gyrinno—friend and lover.

Hector—prince and hero of Troy. Husband to Andromache.

Helen—she of the face "that launched a thousand ships." Wife of Menelaus who ran away with Paris to Ilium (Troy). Menelaus, with his brother Agamemnon as leader, led a coalition of Greek city-states against Troy, a war that lasted ten years. According to many sources, Helen was never at Troy, but stayed in Egypt, waiting for her husband to find her—something he did, according to Euripides, only after the war ended, and the phantom Helen he took from the citadel disappeared back into air.

Hera—sister and wife of Zeus.

Hermione—Helen's daughter.

Irana—friend and lover.

Larichus—a younger brother, thought to be Sappho's favorite. A handsome young man who poured wine for wealthy Mytileneans, earning his sister's pride.

Leda—raped by Zeus in the form of a swan, gave birth to three eggs. Out of two the *Dioscuri*, twin heroes Castor and Pollux, were born. Out of the third came Helen.

Medea—Thracian princess and sorceress, married the hero Jason, who used her magical help to attain the Golden Fleece. Left her home to go to Greece. On Jason's leaving her for a more "proper" wife, she took revenge by killing the would-be-wife and her father, and murdering her own children. She escaped on a chariot that flew into the air.

Megara—friend, lover, student.

Mica—lover, friend, object of jealousy.

Mnasidica—lover, friend.

Phaon—a man renowned for his beauty. It is said he found a rare plant, sea-holly, whose root takes the shape of the male and female genitals. If a man finds a phallic root, he becomes charged with sexual attraction. Others speak of the remarkable decency of his life, a living made by the sea. When an old man Aphrodite came to him, disguised as a human, and asked for transport. He took her where she wanted to go and asked no money. In return, Aphrodite gave him beauty and youth, fell in love with him, and hid the man among the lettuces. It is for love of Phaon that Sappho leapt from the cliff of Leucates and drowned herself.

Polyanax—father of Gorgo or Andromeda?

Priam—king of Troy. Father of fifty children, all of whom died in the Trojan War.

Scamandronoymus—Sappho's father. Other names abound: Scamander, Simon, Eumenus, Eerigyius, Semus, Camon, or Etarchus.

Telesippa—friend and lover.

Zeus—potent father of the Olympian gods.

A NOTE ON THE TRANSLATION

The voice is a ritual only epochs can reveal. Centuries let the husks of personality we hold on to so dearly fall away and leave radiant and bare some truer seed called self. The voice performs the rites of that self—a meter, a dance, a song—keeping alive what otherwise would be lost. Because it is a ritual, another may learn the rites, may perform them. It is as just such a novice I have turned to Sappho's poems, hoping no more than to apprentice myself the rites of her voice, and in performing them as carefully as I can, return to the page that living voice.

To do so has required choices, line by line and poem by poem, large and small. In the few poems time given us complete, those written in the hendecasyllabic meter known as sapphics, I have done my best to approximate the potency of that rhythm. Meter in the ancient world can be thought of both as musical and mystical. Some meters sanctified marriage. Others, like the dithyrambic, drove those who listened and those who sang into fits of religious ecstasy, giving them some aspect of the power of the god they worshipped. Sappho's eponymous meter begins with the fever of heavy stress, then transitions through the middle of the line into a calmer order at the end. It is as if each line begins with the heart startled into a panicked pulse, that then grows accustomed to the startle. The meter lends a physical intimacy, a visceral interiority, felt in the chamber of the body, to Sappho's poems. Your blood flows to her tune, if you let it.

Sappho is a love poet. The war-verse of the epic was written in hexameters, twelve feet per line. Love walks with a wounded foot. Eleven syllables per line, until the adonic, last line of each stanza, wounds the wound, with its five syllable close. We might pause to note how many heroes come to us with wounded feet: Achilles, Oedipus, Philoctetes. We might think of Hermes' winged feet, who takes a running start and leaps into the air before the last foot falls.

To keep a semblance of that meter meant myriad syntactical choices, and in one case, where I could find no other solution, the addition of a phrase to a rightly famous poem, just four syllables, "Now greaves, not grief," as Sappho asks Aphrodite to fight with her. I would like to claim that the words arrived as a kind of revelation, something given to the novitiate of the rites of a singular voice, but maybe that is simply a self-comforting excuse. What is truer to say is that breaking the metric form felt to me a mistake more egregious than adding in those four words to keep whole the shape entire. But I may be wrong, and apologize for the trespass, to Sappho and Aphrodite both.

Ancient Greek is a stunningly compound language, and many words arrive thick with alternate and immediate meanings, as if each word isn't a worker bee, but a hive. Throughout the poems, I've tried to be honest to that thick complexity, letting a moment in any given poem accumulate alternate versions—a flower as seen through the bee's compound eye. The verb δονέω means "shake," and famously describes Eros's sweet-bitter nature. Love shakes me. But deep in the meaning is agitation of another, related kind—the murmur, the buzz, as of a bee. An image can teach us how to listen more fully. "A bee in a blossom buzzes" reminds us that Love's agitation is the worry that widens the wild field entire. It is my hope that such willingness to go astray is a truer path, and that something comes to light in a mistake that can be seen in no other way.

One of the words for *word* in Ancient Greek is ἔπος. It is from it we get *epic*. So it might be seen that every word is in and of itself an epic poem, one we could read, if only we could fully enter the word. Any word will do. It is with that principle in mind I worked to order this collection of Sappho. If a voice can be thought of as a ritual, a life can be considered an epic—and I wanted to offer an ordering of these poems that give some sense of that epic journey any given life is, one that leaves us it leaves most heroes, limping on a wounded foot. There is a motion how the poems move from first to last, from wondrous recognition of the world, through erotic entanglement, to the sanctity of human bonding, to religion, to morals, to age that threatens to tear apart the sanctities we have clung to, and then to death itself, which might teach us—as Sappho hints—to see ourselves as no more than we are.

THE POEMS

bedrock

whisper

walk
so we can see

dear Dawn's
golden arms

harms

soon golden-sandaled Dawn

Queen Dawn

Hesperus, carrying all that day-brightening dawn scatters about,
you bring the sheep, you bring the goat, you bring the child back to her mother.

*

...of all the stars most beautiful...

the stars back away and hide from the lovely
moon's radiant form, when her greater lamp shines
its silver down on the earth

I myself in summer hours wove together flowers

a tender girl plucking the tender flowers

I think I cannot

with two arms

touch the sky

I don't know where I go

my mind is two minds

and longingly I long and searchingly I search...

a door of carved wood

a robe
also
saffron
a purple robe
to cloak
garlands
beauty
Phrygian
purple

...my mother, she gave birth to me,

once said, deep in the gift of her life,
that curls bound into braids by purple thread
are an adornment great as the cosmic orders,

and this remains very true—
but for the girl with hair so golden
that fire twines curiously through it,

crowns of woven flowers
freshly bloomed and blooming yet
are best to wear, headbands tight fit,

rich embroidery from Sardis...
                    ...cities...

she calls out for her child

a robe
necklaces

Gorgo

beautiful, graceful

Andromeda

Atthis: you

                    remember
for in our youth
we did these things

many things and lovely,
                            the city,
and us, sharp as spears

we live

opposite

reckless
men

but I am not one of spiteful
nature—I have a gentle, silent heart…

of you my lovely ones my thoughts can be thought
by no one else

We will give away, father said (but didn't say).

it cannot be
humans working together to get

what can't be guessed at

As the sweet-apple reddens on the high branch,
high on the highest branch, that the apple-pickers forgot—
no, they didn't forget; that apple they could not reach.

dawn

...to see with what eyes?

innocence

earthly bliss

for Sappho

reckless

her prayer

prayer with no law

barely dark

what is this to me—sweetness?—

that grips my life

Call out to her
    all that is no longer held
        solemn rites

    Hera end

        while I still live

Artemis

Medea

the Hold-Fast, Zeus

Son of Leto and also Zeus
obey and come to your secret rites
leave behind the deep woods of Gruneia
for the oracle

sing praise
sister

of Polynaxes' children
to mock the mad one is what I want

Phoebus golden-haired, birthed by the daughter of Coeus,
who lay with the son of cloudy Cronos, great-named god—
but Artemis swears the great oath of the gods—
"Yes, by your head, I swear I will stay a virgin,
unwedded, among the peaks of lonely mountains
hunting. Come, nod your head, promise for my sake."
So she spoke, and the father of the blessed gods nodded.
"Virgin, shooter of deer, fond of the chase, huntress,
gods and men will call you, a worthy name.
Let sweet-limb-loosening Eros never come near…
                                    fearless…

Come here to me from Crete to this temple's chaste
chamber, beside the bent gracious sacred boughs of
your apple grove, altars burning sweet resin,
     smoke of frankincense:

cold water's music flows through apple-branches,
roses—red, cabbage, wild—cast their shadows dark
on the ground, and the quivering leaves shake down
     sleep deep as coma:

green meadow grass by horses grazed, spring flowers
go countless as they grow, and the galling gale
gently blows [
        [

there now you . . .   take with your hand, Cypris,
these golden cups gracefully, mix the nectar
not with water, mix the sweet nectar into
    us, our happiness.

Cyprus or Paphos or Panormus keeps you

Aphrodite
sweet-voiced
throwing
    holding
    I sit
you leap
    sea-foam

Deepthroned darkcarved wood deathless Aphrodite,
wileweaving child of Zeus, I beg, I pray to you
don't hurt me, my thought, let grief never seduce,
    Queen, my shardscared heart,

but come here, if at some time ever you heard
my fool's voice pour out its wine to wet the ground,
then hear me again, and leave your father's home,
    free from its gold confines,

love's chariot yoked: your beautiful sparrows
struggle to bear you swift above the dark earth,
dense cloud of wings wilding against the heavens
    through mid-air, to bring

you down, suddenly here: you, I swear, blessed one,
smiling, a smile on your face neverdying,
asking, "What do you suffer from now, and why
    summon me again,

what want, what better thing in your craving heart
do you wish to see? Who now? Who must I coax
back again to the agony you love? Who,
    Sappho, does you wrong?

And if now she runs away, soon she will chase;
if she refuses gifts, soon she'll bring her own;
if she won't love you, soon she will be longing,
    even if she doèsn't

want to." Come to me now again, save my mind
scathing in thought, win the warloud din of my heart's
endless desire, end it. Now greaves, not grief. You
    be my battlemate.

if I, golden-crowned Aphrodite, could win
the lot cast out from the shook helmet's ringing

they gave me value, made me honored, with gifts
of their hard labor

you give, Andromeda, as lovely as you take

*

for Sappho, the one rich in blessings, Aphrodite

...Andromeda

for Sappho, I love you
Cyprus queen
and yet great
for eyes the shining sun
glory everywhere
and you in Acheron

I spoke in a dream with Cyprogenia.

o dark Dream
you come in sleep and leave
sweet god, but a wondrous, terrible sorrow
has the force to hold apart
I have hope I won't share
never for the blessed gods—hope
this is not their
plaything, toy
may it bloom into being for me
everything

The gods   suddenly   without tears

of Charaxus   Charaxus

Cypris and Nereids, please, allow my brother
to reach me here unharmed, and that all he wants
in his soulswaying nervetouched nevermind heart
    be for him achieved,

loosen his failures, release him from his wrongs,
let him become for his friends grace's delight,
poison to those he hates, and let it not find
    us, distress, again.

That his sister share in his honor, let him
be willing, sorrow's mournful misery . . .
        and earlier grieving

      sound of a single millet-seed
      blame of the city
             not him

      you holy Cypris
      setting evil aside

Charaxus
accused of doing wrong

disgrace

blessed one

from failures, from earlier wrongs, loosen him
                divine retribution] wood
fates] chances   refuge from the wild sea

Cypris, may she discover you most bitter,
Doricha, loud-tongue boaster, may she never
·speak of how, a second time, he came to her,
    longing after love.

Doricha
   come help, don't

a mat of woven reeds, pride
         for young men
  dear one

Sappho to Charaxus

sent   proof   a shared drink

Polyanax

burdens ˈ brightness of living water and / sheen of wine and

with fate being faithful   to lay hold the harbor   dark earth

in marshland the sailors   a great gale   dry land

        sails   the cargo out from

ceaseless flow   of labors on dry land

not the honey nor the honey-bee are mine

and the hyacinth high in the hills the shepherds trampled underfoot
and on the ground, purple flowers...

sprung up from wet dirt gold chickpeas

...they say that Leda found an egg
hidden in wild hyacinth...

far whiter, far brighter, than an egg

Some say cavalry, some spears on foot in form-
ation, some say ships are what on the dark earth
appears most beautiful; but I say beauty
    is whatever you

love. Wholly simple to make all understand
this wisdom: she who far outshone all others
in beauty, Helen, left her noblest-of-
    all-men husband, and

sailed to Troy, no memory whole in her mind,
not of her children, not of dear parents, no—
love misled her

                 . . . lightly
    now Anactoria returns to my mind—
that you are not here.

But I would rather see her lovely walk, would
rather see the bright spark lamp that is her face
than Lydian chariots or the long shields
    foot-soldiers hold in lines.

Near me I'm praying you appear, you reveal your-
self, queen Hera, your grace-bearing form comely,
who the Atridae prayed to, prayed against, those
    men called mighty kings—

keeping the promise of many wretched labors
done, first around Ilium, then in the wild toss
of open sea, this coming-to-anchor path
    unable to end,

until they summoned to presence you and Zeus
and Thyones' longed for, loving child—
now, of gentle spirit, bring your help to me
    as in ancient days

you did. Chaste and beautiful [
maidens [
both [

to be...
    to arrive...

Cypris
the war-herald came   a bird / a song   words
Idaeus gently spoke   swift messenger

—one line missing—

the rest of Asia   fame never dying—
Hector and his shipmates are bringing her of darting-eyes
from holy Thebes and the flowing waters of Placia,
graceful Andromache, in their ship across the salt
of open sea—many bracelets of gold laurel-leaves,
purple robes, delicate trinkets finely construed,
silver wine-cups past counting, and ivory, too.
He spoke—and quickly his loved father leapt up,
his voice crossing the wide city to reach his friends.
Right away the sons of Ilus yoked the mules
to carriages smooth-running, and the whole throng
of woman and maidens tender-ankled at once
clambered on. Apart again the daughters of Priam [
men yoked horses to chariots…
        unmarried youth from far and wide…
    chariot-drivers…

—several lines missing—

                    as gods guiltless
                    move as
one   toward Troy
the pipe's sweet notes and the cithara's meld

with castanet's jangle, virgins singing loud and clear
their song of pure prayer, whose divine utter echo
reaches past the sky...
all is a path / is a way / is a road
the bowls for mixing wine and the ash-bearing urns
myrrh, cinnamon, and frankincense, all mingle—
the old women cry out their praise,
all the men sing with voices sprung from arrow strings
straight to the good-singing-god, Apollo, archer
who aims well his lyre, singing
hymns to godlike Hector and Andromache.

myth-weaver

with many wreaths of many colors
the earth is crowned

I have a child, she is the golden flowers
she seems to be, my only Cleis,
for whom I would not trade the daughters of Lydia,
                              or lovely...

For you, Cleis, with fine embroidery,
I cannot get one,
a headband—but the Mytilenean…

                to have
        the finely fashioned…

these sons of Cleanax
exiled…the same city has burial mounds,
memorials—worn away as if by water

                           she hid
her foot in a leather shoe of many colors,
fine Lydian craft

I would not think a girl, eyes testing the light of the sun,
to have such wisdom, not ever, not now, not at any
   time

a dress

leather of many colors

purse / vainbag

and also of hand-towels…
purple, scented…
sent from Phoceas..
a costly gift…

a linen towel dripping wet

washing-soda

Sweet mother, I cannot weave at the loom—
love seduced me, slender Aphrodite's fault.

Love shook frantic
my heart, wind crashes down on mountain oaks

Mnasidica's body more shapely than soft Gyrinno…

on soft cushions I will lay
calm my limbs

sleeping on the breast of your soft companion

Is it for virginity I lust?

I loved you, Atthis, long ago…

a small child you seemed to me, without grace

What country girl charms your mind…
wearing country clothes…
not knowing how to pull her pants over her ankles…

you are yourself, Calliope

you I sought, you came,
and cooled my heart longing thoughts enflamed

Stand before me, you I love,
and spread out the grace from your eyes.

the peace-of-no-desire at war again
troubles the frantic heart / mind toils
　and takes a seat
but come, you loved ones
　day nears

desiremind / passionsoul
                gather all
I dare,

        my
flame by other flame lit
        face

your light touch

> often
>> for that one
> I shine bright, but those I love better than all
>> hurt me most
>>> idle vanity
>
>>> I in truth myself
> know this guilty thing

arriving by chance
I want the girl who actually exists
ending as a thought
for years I call out
in my heart suddenly quick
that you gain as much as you wish
to fight for me [with me
faith in our fragile luxuries
you know so well

Love, now again, limb-loosener, shakes my mind,
   [a bee in a blossom buzzes [
that sweet-bitter beast no one can battle

I honestly wish I'd died—
she left me behind, weeping

much, and said this to me:
"What fears we've suffered,
Sappho, I leave you against my will."

I answered her:
"Go in joy, and remember me,
know that we loved you.

If not, then you I want
to remind…
            …what beauty we bore.

Many wreaths of violets,
of roses threaded with crocus,
you made with me and wore,

and many garlands, coiled
around tender necks,
you made, of woven flowers,

and doused in sweet perfume
costly…
as would coat a queen,

and spread out on soft beds
so tender…
you satisfied your desire,

there was none, not one
shrine
from which we were missing,

no sacred grove, no dance,
                not even a sound…"

ran
like fawns
sent forth
the golden
mind
in need

for me away from those
    yet became
        equal with the gods
          sinning
Andromeda
             blessed happiness
      character's trope
from bliss-tired laze not holding back
    sons of Tyndareus
            full of grace
  innocent no longer
Megara peaceful and still

] from love, hope

    ...that against another, when I look at you,
Hermione herself appears less than she is,
and to say you are like gold-silk haired Helen
    is not said in shame

    ...mortal women, this you was your own,
    playing as a child plays with my worry-worn mind,

          river banks wet with dew

          awake all through the holy night

Sardis…
often her mind holds her here…

how   we thought
you a goddess, you seemed a goddess, so easily
known, delighting most in the dance.

Now among the Lydian women you shine
brightest, as the sun
sets and rose-fingers catch the moon,

outshines all the stars—and that light
flowing out over the sea's field of salt, flows
down on the wildflowers in the furrow;

dew hangs down, ripe with beauty,
budding on tender roses,
parsley, and the blooming clover.

Often, she wanders, remembering
gentle Atthis, desire
husking her heart thin at your fate—

to go there…   this not
known…   so much
sings praise…   in the midst of…

it is no easy thing, to equal goddesses
in the body's beauty…

and...   Aphrodite...

                    ...you pour wine
into golden cups...
        ...your hands, those gods, Persuasion

…golden cups…

drop by drop, in my pain

*

let winds and sorrows bear away the one
who refused me

but if at me
you gazed, behold—
it's grown—
wealth the gods give

He appears to me as do those blessed gods,
that man, that one man, who sits facing you,
sits close, sits near, listens to the articulate
    music of your voice

and the longing alive inside your laughter—
struck-by-terror it's true, this heart in my breast.
Glimpsing you but for a second unvoices me,
    speech impossible,

my tongue a boat-broken wave, some fire's thin husk
burns its fine edge beneath my skin, as if blind,
my open eyes see nothing, some hum, some buzz,
    is all I can hear,

sweat pours off me like water as if I toiled
long, like a child, trembling takes hold of me,
more green than grass is green, I seem to myself
    almost dying to die...

...but the heart endures all, poor day-laborer...

labor
     a face closely watched
   stays hidden

   the human voice
  if not, winter
    numb pain

     I command you, sing
Abanthi to Gongyla, take knowingly in hand…
make peace, while between you and you desire flies,
   a bird in circles,

   to beauty—the drape of her dress
made you stumble when you saw it, and I rejoice—
for the pure born Cyprian herself once blamed
   even my prayer

to win her…
this shape…
I want…

                      Mica
           but you I will not suffer
       those most-loved you seized for yourself
                           from the house of Penthilus
                   malign creature
a song sweet in the mouth
           soft-voiced
singing, clear as nightingale and bitterly
                           covered in dew

striking the gut-strings of the lyre
with a dildo it seems
at a kind touch
she quivers

don't fool around with the rubble

the river left behind

but you never cause disdain, Irana

Why me, Irana? The daughter of Pandion, the swallow, her twittering…

...so often I say hello to the daughter of Polynax

scared you cowered…
sweet bay tree when…
all that pleased the tongue…
than that one…
and with the…
traveler of open roads…
scarcely I heard…
beloved holy soul…
such is now…
to have craved gentleness…
come before others—beauty…
and clothes…

The door-keeper's feet are seven fathom's long,
his sandals made from the hides of five ox,
and ten sandal-makers toiling hard made them.

Leto and Niobe are very loving friends.

...and my Archeanassa
...Gorgo's yoke-mate

we've had more than our fill

Gorgo

Gongyla

my loved one

honey-voiced girl

for as long as you want

…and with wool fine-woven, tucked her in tightly.

coming down from heaven
in a tattered purple cloak

...you and my servant Eros...

over flames you sear us

bringer of pain

Girlhood, virginity, how did you leave me, where did you go?
I will never return to you, never come back.

lovely-voiced messenger, the nightingale

Come, tortoise-shell lyre, and speak through me—
give birth to yourself in a song.

For servants of the Muses, it is not just
for lament to live in the house: for us this dirge isn't right.

...Muses bright
...builds and of the Graces
...for the mind goes slow
...lust is a sacred grove don't forget
...mortals share

As superior as are the singers of Lesbos to those from other lands…

a singing far sweeter than the lyre's...
more golden than gold...

...armed with bruised roses, pure Graces,
daughters of Zeus, come here...

                    set aside
                    most swiftly

you, Dica, with garlands crowning your lovely curls,
sprigs of dill tied together by your tender hands—
what arrives in flowers the blessed Graces
most adore, from the uncrowned they turn away

Be here again, Muses, leave behind your golden…

...from the Muses...

honey-voiced

soft-voiced

...come now, delicate Graces
and Muses with your beautiful hair...

...now for these friends
I will sing my lovely songs for their delight.

...and once you were a child
...come and sing these things
...praise, and
...give us love's fine favors—

for we're walking to a wedding, fine indeed...
and this you know, but unless quickly...
you shoo the virgins away, the gods...
　　...the gods have [the gods are holding

　　　　　...the shining path to Olympus
　　　　　　...for men doesn't exist

night

virgins
night-long
full-of-song might sing the most loved young
bride dressed in violets...

...rouse the boys not married,
go, and walk with the youth your own age, that we
might see in their eyes less sleep than the nightingale,
    clear-voiced bird, should know.

Raise high the roof-beam,
Hymenaeus,
Builders, raise it high,
Hymenaeus,
The bridegroom enters, equal to Ares,
A man more mighty than mighty men.

ambrosia
mixed in a mixing-bowl,
which Hermes took and for the gods poured out
the wine, they all
held drinking cups,
poured a libation, prayed all together for the good
bridegroom

Blessed bridegroom, the wedding you've prayed for
has come to be, you have that girl for whom you prayed...
her graceful form, the idea of her holds grace, her eyes...
are gentle, and the love you longed for pours out her face...
           ...she had honored you, Aphrodite

Now there was no other girl, bridegroom, as this one.

And to what lovely thing, lovely bridegroom, can I compare you?
A slender sapling, that draws you best.

Go rejoicing, bride; leave in joy, bridegroom!

guard over her   bridegroom   king of cities

...the bedroom
....the bride's beautiful feet

        I swear
and this…

lament of the half-divine
unloved
and for now
no cause
nothing much

idle   even in sacrifice   holding faith

if stepping down   we see in mind   labors

behind us   this saying

I came

for harmony
to choir of much delight
clear-voiced

full of a river's peace
   aegis-bearing
      Cytherea I utter the prayers
   that hold my heart
hear me now and one of these...
      abandoning
        my
         difficult grief

full and satisfied the moon rose,
women gathered around the altar

to you I give
a goat pure white

I want to say one thing, but shame
stops me...

If you longed for the faithful and beautiful,
and your tongue wasn't stirring up evil to speak,
if shame didn't fill your eyes blind,
then what you said would do justice.

All   telling   tongue
A myth word for word   and a man   greater

When in the fertile breast anger is sown,
guard the tongue's idle barking.

Money minus virtue is no harmless neighbor,
But both intermixed, you hold on the happiness's height.

His body is beautiful, as far as beauty goes,
But he who is good is beauty embodied.

…he thinks of himself…

much-too-knowing

give

of many glories / of much renown
of beauties, of nobilities, you
with friends, grieving also
you chastise me

engorged
you glut . . . my thoughts
not this
should be turned towards

never   thirst's lifeless groan
I should understand
was most evil

for one or for others
hearts / minds, well-

blessed ones / gods

                    before...
                    toward when...

                    you could wish
                            so little
                            to be borne
                                what [who
my   sweet
of the   you had known yourself
and   I've forgotten
you
or   someone could speak
                                    also I...
I'll love   as long as breath is in me
                                will weigh thought down
                                a friend I said becomes strong

        troubles
    sharp-edged

        this you were...
            you...
                but I will love...
                what
        is better
            than arrows

all night long they leave her alone

their hearts grew cold,
    limp wings no strength to fly

Atthis, thinking of me you hate
the thought, and to Andromeda fly away.

and like an old man…

danger…

...down-blowing

But if you are my friend,
your bed will win over a younger woman—
for I cannot endure living
together as one, being the older.

let loose] fallen down] caught the mind's attention
   loud-voiced lament
for fear trembling   but

     my skin, old age already
      she embraces
    startled, darts away

     the noble women
      understand
    wind-blown mind sings
her clothed in purple

      what's best
      wanders

over-powering [or running away
was taught [was bitten
but others
sat [or words flowed out
you own your name
put in the mouth the seizure starts
the beautiful gifts of children
the loved singer sings love clear on turtle-shell lyre
but all my skin already old
my dark hair turning white
knees not bearing
with only a fawn's strength
but what could I do—
no power to become
rose-armed Dawn
carrying to the earth's very end
took hold of him
an immortal wife
deems worthy
might grant one to follow
I kiss glory   and this, for me—
the lamp-bright beauty of the sun—
love has gotten.

Someone keeps us in mind
I say
        in time yet to come

You have forgotten me

*

Some other man, instead of me, you love

The moon rose
and the Pleiades—mid-
night, the hours do their work,
and I sleep alone.

He is dying, Cythera, lovely Adonis, what do we do?
Strike your breasts, girls, tear apart your clothes.

O, Adonis

Gongyla

an omen
for a child mostly, Hermes
arrived

I said, "O despot,
I swear by the blessed ones
I've taken no pleasure being on earth,

and some desire to be dead has hold of me,
to see the lotus-covered, wet with dew,
banks of the river Acheron."

Being dead in that place, where there is no memory of you,
where no one's longing follows after you, for you have no
    share in Pierian roses,
but flung from us, dumb in Hades home-school, on infinite
repeat, taking your lessons among the dimly-seen dead.

...shallow enough to cross...

…I might go…

…I might bring with me…

...no one   Sappho   no one...

…Sappho…

…with eyes gone night-dark too early…

... more green
than grass I am, dying
just a little from needing
so much, so I see me
as I am—myself...

DAN BEACHY-QUICK is the author, most recently, of a collection of essays, fragments, and poems, *Of Silence & Song* (Milkweed, 2017). He has written six books of poetry, *gentlessness, Circle's Apprentice, North True South Bright, Spell, Mulberry*, and *This Nest, Swift Passerine*, six chapbooks, *Shields & Shards & Stitches & Songs, Apology for the Book of Creatures, Overtakelessness, Heroisms, Canto* and *Mobius Crowns* (the latter two both written in collaboration with the poet Srikanth Reddy), a book of interlinked essays on *Moby-Dick, A Whaler's Dictionary,* as well as a collection of essays, meditations and tales, *Wonderful Investigations*. Reddy and Beachy-Quick's collaboration has recently been released as a full-length collection, *Conversities*, and he has also collaborated with the essayist and performance artist Matthew Goulish on *Work From Memory*. In 2013, University of Iowa Press published a monograph on John Keats in their Muse Series (editor Robert D. Richardson) titled *A Brigh ter Word Than Bright: Keats at Work*, and Coffee House Press published his first novel, *An Impenetrable Screen of Purest Sky*. He is a contributing editor for the journals *A Public Space* and *West Branch*. After graduating from the University of Denver, he attended the Iowa Writer's Workshop. He has taught at Grinnell College, The School of the Art Institute of Chicago, and is currently teaching in the MFA Writing Program at Colorado State University. His work has been a winner of the Colorado Book Award, and has been a finalist for the William Carlos Williams Prize, and the PEN/USA Literary Award in Poetry. He is the recipient of a Lannan Foundation residency, and taught as Visiting Faculty at the Iowa Writer's Workshop in spring 2010. He was one of two Monfort Professors at CSU for 2013-2015, and has been a Guggenheim Fellow and a Creative Fellow of the Woodberry Poetry Room at Harvard University.